MY PEOPLE

A catalogue record for this book is available from the British Library.

First published in Great Britain in 2022
by Carpet Bombing Culture.
An imprint of Pro-actif Communications.

Email: books@carpetbombingculture.co.uk

Written by Patrick Potter and Gary Shove

ISBN: 978-1-908211-91-0

www.carpetbombingculture.com

WELCOME

...TO THE MOST PRECIOUS BOOK
YOU WILL EVER OWN.

My name is

....

but you can call me

....

Today is

....

and I am going to get my people
to fill the pages of this book
by the following date

....

I got this book from

....

When it is finished I will

....

....

....

....

....

This is

'MY PEOPLE'

- a unique time capsule of your friends
that you can treasure forever.

It's a **guided journal** reimagined as a **group project**.

Capture the unique micro-universe
that you create with your inner circle
of favourite people.

Because **our minds are made
of the people we grew up with.**

GET YOUR CLOSEST FRIENDS
TO WRECK THIS BOOK,
...THEN KEEP IT FOREVER.

BURY AFTER WRITING.

Fresh from the factory,

this book is identical to a million others.

But with just **one scribble**, from **one friend**,

it becomes **instantly unique**.

...And that's real magic.

The moment your friends put pen to paper,

they transform this book into a **real treasure**.

Something you will carry with you through

all the chapters of your life.

BETTER
THAN
HYPERREAL.

Real touch, real handwriting, real moments.
That's the old magic,
the old 'lock-of-hair-voodoo' of physical contact.
Atoms intermingling. The sacred analogue.

This is way better than feeding your life
to the algorithms, pixel by pixel,
waiting for the robots to auto-generate your nostalgia.

THIS IS
REAL LIFE.

BUT
MY FRIENDS
HATE WRITING!

Don't worry, it's dead easy.
Some options are so easy you literally just tick boxes,
and some options allow more space
for self-expression. Some friends will want to do
a little, some will want to do a lot.
There's something for everyone.

ANYWAY, WHO DOESN'T LOVE TALKING ABOUT THEMSELVES?

Just pick your moment
and hand them the book and a pen.

WARNING:

If someone writes
in your book you are sworn
to one day return the favour.

THE RULES:

- Let them pick their own page spread.

- Make sure they sign and date their contributions.

- Ignore the rules.

BUT I ONLY LIKE THREE HUMANS IN THIS WHOLE CURSED WORLD.

You can get a small group of people
to fill in the whole book at intervals
over a longer time or you can get lots of
different people to fill it in over a shorter time,
or any combination of the above.
Whatever works.

EVEN HALF-FINISHED
IT WILL BE PRICELESS.

Keep it in your bag and just keep adding to it
until it gets full. It will be fascinating to track
the changes in your friendship group over time.
Little by little, it will fill up.

And it will capture the spirit of a chapter of your life.

Imagine how much it will mean to you
in say five, ten or even twenty years time.

YOU KNOW
WHAT TO DO.

'This book' + 'your friends' + 'a pen'
= treasure

What song would you choose to be the theme tune to your life?

Interesting job with low pay or a boring job with high pay?

You are having a fantasy game night.
You can invite 5 people dead or alive from any time in history:

(1)

(2)

(3)

(4)

(5)

What games are you playing?

LIKES & DISLIKES

Complete with a friend. Start by filling the centre overlap area with things you both like, then find things that only one of you likes and fill in the top and bottom areas. If you're stuck for ideas, start with food...

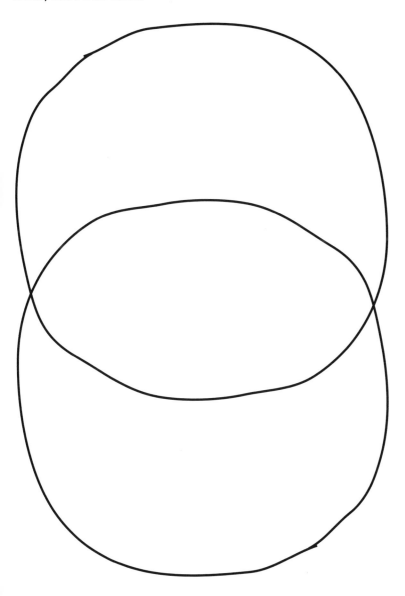

They are making a movie about you and your closest circle of friends.

- What is your quest?

- Who is the bad guy?

- What happens at the climax?

- What song plays over the end credits?

- Which actors play you and your friends?

List four things that mean something to you:

A place

A movie

A book

An object

Who would you like to swap places with for a day?

A famous writer has written a smash hit novelisation of your life, what is it called?

One thing . . .

You need

You want

That makes you happy

That makes you angry

If you could put one message on a giant digital billboard in Times Square what would it say?

If you were forced to sing karaoke what song would you choose?

Doodle a self portrait with your eyes closed.

Create a list of things that you want to do before you are 30.

If money were no object but you could buy only one thing,
what would you choose?

What is the weirdest thing that you've ever eaten?

What book had the most influence on you?

If all jobs paid the same, what would be your dream job?

Who is your hero?

Things that I will never do (tick those that apply).

○ Go to the movies alone

○ Start a YouTube channel

○ Make a Tik-Tok video

○ Join a gym

○ Run a marathon

○ Read a book

○ Do the dishes

○ Ghost someone

○ Start a journal

What is one thing that makes you angry right now?

Who was your first crush?

What image are you currently using as your cellphone wallpaper?

You inherit a million, what's on your shopping list?

What are you currently:

Feeling

Planning

Loving

Hating

What's your Saturday night going out song?

What's the hardest thing you've ever done?

Name one thing in society that you think is broken?

If you were given an envelope and inside was written the date and time of your death, would you open it?

Draw the first image that enters your head RIGHT NOW.

You are given control of your country for one day and you can change anything. What do you do?

Most Likely.

It's like a yearbook but it's better because you actually choose what goes into it.

Write one name for each:

Most likely to join the circus

Most likely to write a bestseller

Most likely to be a billionaire

Most likely to win an Oscar

Most likely to be on the cover of a magazine

Most likely to be a famous artist

Think how you feel right now emotionally. Now doodle a self-portrait using only scribbles. If you feel irritable or angry, doodle quickly and furiously, if you're feeling chilled and relaxed, doodle slowly and smoothly. Try to doodle your features so that they represent how you feel right now.

List your favourite:

TV series

YouTuber

Actor

City

Artist

Divulge one thing about you that might surprise people.

If you could click your fingers and travel to any place in the world right now, where would you go?

Doodle some faces.

Create the name for a new fashion brand.

Either / Or - Circle your choice

Lead or Follow

Comedy Film or Thriller Film

Live in Asia or Live in Africa

Go forward in time 50 years or Go Back in time 100 years

Starter or Dessert

Thrift Store or Chain Store

Work hard or Hardly work

Head or Heart

Find your soulmate or Win the lottery

Create a new language and write a sentence here that only you will ever understand.

Create a self-portrait using 'blind contour doodling'. Look into a mirror, or into a selfie cam, but do not look at the paper and do not lift your pen from the paper. Start by sketching the outline of your head and go from there.
Do not look at the drawing until it is finished.

You've won the holiday of a lifetime, choose ONE destination from anywhere in the world.

Imagine you have started your own successful business, what does it do?

List three things that you are good at:

(**1**)

(**2**)

(**3**)

If you had to pass yourself off as an expert, what would the topic be?

BINGO

Read the bingo card. If something is true for you, then put a big cross in the box. If you get a line of four crosses in any direction, shout BINGO!*

Have taken a selfie in the last 24 hours	Have a turntable	Shop at thrift stores	Are always late
Post food pics on instagram	Have a gym membership	Have a part-time job	Love Hip Hop
Would rather text than call	In a relationship	Have never read a book in the past year	Have a side hustle
Worry about global warming	Are always broke	Have quit a job	Have used coupons

You are put in charge of the country for one day, place these issues in order of importance:

a) Gun control ⭕

b) Tax policy ⭕

c) Education ⭕

d) Health and social care ⭕

e) Climate change ⭕

f) Law and order policy ⭕

g) Defence spending ⭕

h) Drug and alcohol policy ⭕

*Sorry there is no prize.

You can only choose one. You lose the rest forever.
Circle your choice.

Playstation

Xbox

Nintendo

Steam

itch.io

Mobile Gaming

What is your generation's hope?

Name one thing that you will not eat under any
circumstances.

Get some ink on your fingertips and make a set of prints here.

Imagine it's time to choose your career and only the following options are available, which one do you pick?

Vet	○	Lawyer	○
Chef	○	Journalist	○
City Trader	○	Airline Pilot	○
Actor	○	Hairstylist	○
Counsellor	○	Massage Therapist	○
Web developer	○	Dog Groomer	○
Dentist	○	Mortician	○

Best road trip ever...

- Who is in the car?:

- Who is driving the car?:

- What are you driving?:

- Where are you going?:

What is your favourite brand?

Where do you want to be in ten years time?

Doodle one thing that you want RIGHT NOW.

On a scale of 1 to 10.
Mark a cross along the line between two opposing adjectives.
Where are you on the spectrum?

Conservative ·· Liberal

Binary ·· Non-Binary

Romantic ·· Cynical

Spontaneous ·· Reliable

Intuitive ·· Analytical

Creative ·· Scientific

Aloof ·· Aggressive

Impulsive ·· Controlled

Thrifty ·· Extravagant

Patient ·· Impatient

What's your go-to motivational song?

Describe in one word, 'life without the internet'.

Either / Or - Circle your choice.

Rich and Lonely or Poor and Loved

Slacker or Over-achiever

Truth or Dare

Going out or Staying in

More time or More money

Time travel or Space Travel

Test the waters or Dive in the deep end

Play sport or Watch sport

List three things that put a smile on your face:

(**1**)

(**2**)

(**3**)

Create the name for a new style of music .

What's your strongest talent?

In 10 years what will you be...

Buying

Learning

Focussed on

Name your guilty pleasure.

Recommend a TV series to binge watch.

Doodle a self portrait using only letters from the alphabet. Use lots of different letters, lowercase and capitals, of different sizes and styles to sketch out your face.

List your three greatest fears.

(1)

(2)

(3)

Rank these in terms of the biggest influences on your behaviour and actions:

Generation   ( )

Personality   ( )

Parents   ( )

Social Class   ( )

Gender Identity   ( )

Sexuality   ( )

Nationality   ( )

Religion/beliefs   ( )

Describe education in one word.

List three attributes that you look for in the perfect partner.

①

②

③

If you knew that you could not fail, what would you do?

What is the last thing that made you laugh out loud?

What cause are you most passionate about?

Best party ever...

- Where is it hosted?:

- Who is organising it?:

- Who is doing the music?:

- What is the theme?:

- Everyone goes crazy when:

One thing that only you and your friends would find funny.

Doodle using as many different tools, pens, pencils, highlighters, corrective fluid, make-up, paint, teabags, crayons or whatever you can find.

How would you describe yourself to other people using only 3 words?

List your favourite:

Song

Celebrity

Fictional character

Drink

Sport

Brand

Doodle a self-portrait using only dashes (-). The dashes can be different sizes and of different thickness. Illustrate your mood by adding words that express how you feel right now.

FRIENDS FOREVER?

Ever since classic 1990s TV show 'Friends' was first aired, people have invested time in deciding which characters best represent their real life friends.

- Who in your group is Chandler?:

- Who in your group is Monica?:

- Who in your group is Phoebe?:

- Who in your group is Ross?:

- Who in your group is Rachel?:

- Who in your group is Joey?:

Draw a portrait without ever taking the pen or pencil off the page.

Have you ever nearly died?

Five reasons why you are friends with the owner of this book.

(**1**)

(**2**)

(**3**)

(**4**)

(**5**)

What do you do when you're in town?

Name your favourite teacher.

Finish these sentences . . .

Never have I ever...

The one thing in the world that I cannot live without is...

Last night I...

The key to happiness is...

Most Likely.

It's like a yearbook but it's better because you actually choose what goes into it.

Write one name for each:

Most likely to be a teacher

Most likely to buy a one way ticket to Mars

Most likely to get married first

Most likely to rule the world

Most likely to get arrested

Most likely to become CEO of a multi-national company

Doodle a map of your social world, put the thickest lines between the strongest relationships.

The owner of this book is your...

friend / relative / classmate / colleague / roommate / partner /
alter-ego / sibling / mother / father / grandparent / carer / pet /
manager / life coach / therapist
(strike out as appropriate)

**Write one word here that expresses exactly how you feel
right now.**

You can keep only 3:
Circle your choices.

Jazz / Hip Hop / K-Pop / Electro / Heavy Rock / Country / Jazz
/ Punk / Soul / Classical / Techno / Dubstep / Indie / Dance /
Pop Music / Folk / Electronic / Grime / R&B / Reggae /
Ambient / Drum & Bass / Trance

**If you could only eat at one restaurant for the rest of your life,
which one would it be?**

Name one thing that you just don't get.

Doodle whatever you normally doodle when you're bored.

What are the sacred texts?

(Not just books, a 'sacred text' could be any piece of culture that is deeply important to your inner circle, for example a movie, or even a thread on social media.) **Make a list here:**

Doodle your spirit animal.

List your favourite:

Movie

Book

DJ

Colour

Word

Celebrity crush

Doodle a self portrait using only numbers. Use lots of different numbers, of different sizes and styles, to sketch out your face.

Circle the answer that you agree with:

I am always prepared:	True	Sometimes	Never
I am a pessimist:	True	Sometimes	Never
I get stressed easily:	True	Sometimes	Never
I feel that I am better than other people:	True	Sometimes	Never
If I make plans I like to stick to them:	True	Sometimes	Never
I have a vivid imagination:	True	Sometimes	Never
I put others before myself:	True	Sometimes	Never
I make friends easily:	True	Sometimes	Never

Where do you find people like you on the internet?

What is your favourite movie quote?

BINGO

Read the bingo card. If something is true for you, then put a big cross in the box. If you get a line of four crosses in any direction, shout BINGO!*

Romantic	Ambitious	Religious / spiritual	Shy
Sporty	Picky	Forgetful	Political
Sarcastic	Sensitive	Uninhibited	Competitive
Untidy	Opinionated	Rebellious	Impulsive

What do you do normally do on the weekend?

Write down the first three letter word that comes to mind.

*Sorry there is no prize.

Best gap year ever...

- Where are you going?:

- Who is with you?:

- What's on the to do list?:

Name one thing that stresses you out?

Scribble up a scribble portrait. Express your mood creatively by doodling and adding words and images.

What do you typically do at parties?

A famous songwriter has written a hit song about you, what is it called?

Rate your life...

Mark a cross on the line that shows where you sit.

Self control	low ··	high
Stress level	low ··	high
Love of money	low ··	high
Intelligence	low ··	high
Looks	low ··	high
Work Ethic	low ··	high
Imagination/creativity	low ··	high
Love life	low ··	high
Boredom threshold	low ··	high

Think your happy thoughts and doodle freely for three minutes. See what comes out...

Confess. Name one skeleton to be found in your closet.

What do you do in the evening?

What's your favourite game?

Describe a typical Sunday morning.

You can only choose one. You lose the rest forever.
Circle your choice.

Amazon Prime

Netflix

Disney Plus

HBO Max

Hulu

Discovery+

ESPN+ / Sky Sports

Crunchyroll

Twitch

YouTube

Describe in one word what your relationship with your closest friends looks like to other people.

What's your favourite conspiracy theory?

Most Likely.

It's like a yearbook but it's better because you actually choose what goes into it.

Write one name for each:

Most likely to join a cult

Most likely to have their own reality show

Most likely to lead a protest

Most likely to be an influencer

Most likely to marry someone they just met

Most likely to top the charts

Doodle a self portrait using only arrows. They can be different sizes, different thicknesses and point in different directions.

Describe the moment you first realised you were going to be friends with the owner of this book.

In 10 years where will you be . . .

Living

Working

Holidaying

Describe a moment when it felt like you were physically linked with a close friend.

Write a haiku. Three short lines that do not rhyme. Typically, the first line should have 5 syllables, the second 7 and the last 5. The third line should contain some kind of surprise change of tone.

Either / Or - Circle your choice.

Reactive or **Proactive**

Optimist or **Pessimist**

Think out loud or **Think in your head**

Practical or **Imaginative**

Neat or **Messy**

Introvert or **Extrovert**

How do you think people describe you when you're not around?

One thing . . .

You cannot get enough of

That you want less of

That bores you

That you are fearful of

What was the last thing that you showed someone on your cellphone?

**They are making a movie about you
and your closest circle of friends.**

- Which actor plays the part of you?

- What song plays over the opening titles?

- Who is the enemy?

- What's the twist ending?

What's your leadership style?
Circle your choice:

Do as I say / Let's do it together / You tell me / We'll vote on it /
Do what you want / Just do it

There can be only one social media platform.
Choose one:

What are the top five things that you talk about when you're with your closest friends?

(1)

(2)

(3)

(4)

(5)

Either / Or - Circle your choice.

Early Bird or Night Owl

Long Walks or Long Talks

Live in Europe or Live in USA

Horror Film or Rom Com

Spend or Save

In store or On line

Fiction or Non-fiction

Name one thing or person that motivates you to succeed.

BELIEFS.

Complete with a friend. Start by filling the centre overlap area with things you both like, then find things that only one of you likes and fill in the top and bottom areas. Here are some prompts to get you started:

God / Gods / The Goddess / Ghosts / Life After Death / Aliens
Poltergeists / Mediums / Psychics / Faith healing / Fairies /
Angels / Spirit guides / Trickle down economics

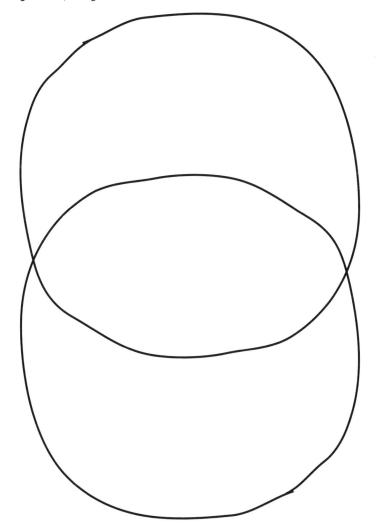

What are your top five fears right now?

1

2

3

4

5

How did the owner of this book persuade you to write in it?
(Delete as appropriate).

hype / coercion / blackmail / bribery / trade / persuasion /
nagging / mild violence / hypnosis / other (describe)

When did you last laugh until you cried?

Make 3 predications about the future:

①

②

③

Name one person you want to punch in the face.

Either / Or - Circle your choice.

Dogs or Cats

City or Country

Barbecue or Pizza Oven

Beach or Mountains

Movies or Music

Bathtub or Shower

Ghosts or Aliens

Theme Park or Water Park

Rank these in terms of the biggest influences on your behaviour and actions:

Psychology   ○

Information Environment ○

Physical Health   ○

Nationality   ○

Beliefs   ○

Material Wealth   ○

Parents   ○

Friends   ○

Imagine you need to start a side hustle to create some extra spending money, what are you going to do?

What is your favourite bird?

Doodle something that represents your favourite song of all time.

Which generation do you identify as being from?

- baby boomer
- generation x
- millennial
- generation z
- generation alpha
- other (please describe)

Recommend one movie.

Which historical period would suit you the best?

List 3 things that you are obsessed with:

Doodle your self portrait using your non-dominant hand.

List your top 3 songs of all time:

(**1**)

(**2**)

(**3**)

Do you identify with your contemporaries, or feel like you're in the wrong timeline?

What is the one thing that you think you will always be remembered for?

If you could ask your future self one question what would it be?

SKILLS & TALENTS

Complete with a friend. Start by filling the centre overlap area with things you both like, then find things that only one of you likes and fill in the top and bottom areas. If you're stuck for ideas, maybe start with school subjects...

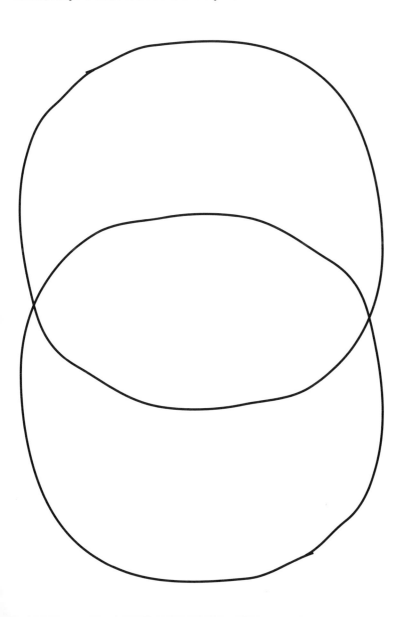

Plan a Fantasy Dinner Party.

Pick five guests (dead or alive / from any time in history):

(1)

(2)

(3)

(4)

(5)

Where is it taking place?

Who is providing the evening's entertainment?

What are you eating for a starter?

What are you eating for the main course?

What are you eating for dessert?

What's on the drinks trolley?

What genre of music are you playing?

What are the after-dinner games?

How do you feel about higher education?

a) It's a privilege not a right

b) It's a total waste of money

c) Everyone should take advantage of the opportunity

d) I can't think past today

e) Occupy the universities!

If you were transported back 10 years in time what would you say to your younger self?

What does your generation do which the next generation will find hilarious?

Doodle a self-portrait as a caricature. If you're stuck for inspiration try making your head larger than your body or accentuate any part of your body that you feel resonates with you.

Things I will never do (tick those that apply)...

Use a bath bomb ○

Snoop through a friends phone ○

Write poetry ○

Go on a dating app ○

Get a piercing ○

Go hunting ○

Play golf ○

Drink wine ○

Cheat on someone ○

Vape ○

Have cosmetic surgery ○

If you could change one thing about yourself, what would it be?

If you could click your fingers and time-travel to any period in history right now, what time period would you choose?

Doodle something that you love.

List the things that you are currently:

Watching

Reading

Listening to

Craving

How is your generation going to do things differently?

Doodle a self portrait using only squiggly lines. The lines can be different sizes and of different thickness.

List your favourite

Band

TikTok Channel

Food

Place

Film

Activity/hobby

Who would play you in the movie version of your life?

BINGO

Read the bingo card. If something is true for you, then put a big cross in the box. If you get a line of four crosses in any direction, shout BINGO!*

Are a control freak	Have made a bucket list	Have more than 5 close friends	Believe in the reincarnation
Are way too active on social media	Have a messy bedroom	Always root for the hero	Don't have a passport
Play for a team	Don't like exercise	Likes cats	Have more than 2 siblings
Have ridden a horse	Always root for the villain	Have a tidy bedroom	Have dyed hair

Three words to describe your generation:

The meaning of life is:

On a scale of 1 to 10.

Mark a cross along the line between two opposing adjectives. Where are you on the spectrum?

Private	·································	Open
Gay	·································	Straight
Curious	·································	Cautious
Organised	·································	Disorganised
Passive	·································	Active
Conventional	·································	Original
Decisive	·································	Procrastinator
Brainy	·································	Brawny
Self-contained	·································	Sociable
Funny	·································	Serious

Recommend one book.

What do you do when you're bored?

Doodle a self portrait using only circles. The circles can be different sizes and of different thickness.

Good news first or Bad news first?

If you could switch places with one famous person in history, who would you pick?

Finish these sentences . . .

The future is...

I get really angry when...

I don't want to...

Name one thing that you are insanely good at.

If you had your own boat what would you christen it?

SOFT SKILLS.

Rate yourself out of 10 for each of the following soft skills.

- Motivation   ◯ out of 10
- Negotiation   ◯ out of 10
- Empathy   ◯ out of 10
- Small Talk   ◯ out of 10
- Debate   ◯ out of 10
- Assertiveness   ◯ out of 10
- Reflection   ◯ out of 10
- Accepting Criticism   ◯ out of 10
- Taking Compliments   ◯ out of 10
- Organisation   ◯ out of 10

What song do you and your friends know all the words to?

3 things on your bucket list:

(**1**)

(**2**)

(**3**)

List the things that you are currently...

Wanting

Needing

Bored with

Missing

If you were to be famous in the future, what do you think it would be for?

If you could gain one skill, quality or ability, what would you want it to be?

You can keep only 3:
Circle your choices.

Netflix / Cinema / Music / MTV / Facebook / Twitter / Snapchat / Tic Tok / Instagram / What'sApp / Xbox / Nintendo / Playstation / Cellphone

Fill this space with the words only your generation uses.

Describe your dream year of travelling with your core group.

Where would you go together?

How would you travel?

What would go wrong?

What would go right?

What is your most treasured memory?

Fill this space with a list of all of the people and places that influence who you are.

If you could ask a crystal ball to tell you the truthful answer to any question, what would you want to know?

One thing...

You believe in

You want to try

You don't want to do

That you love

Write a secret message in mirror writing.

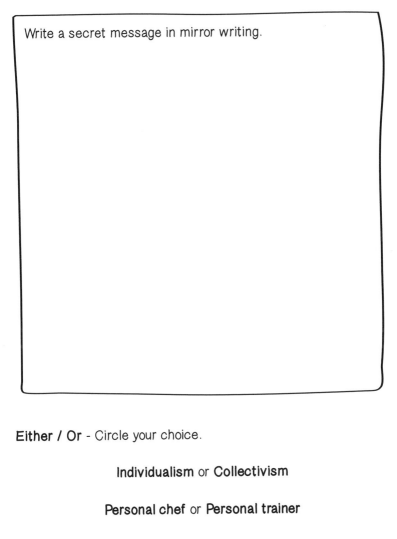

Either / Or - Circle your choice.

Individualism or Collectivism

Personal chef or Personal trainer

Ambitious or Laid back

Romantic or Realistic

Original designer fashion or Fake designer fashion

Spontaneity or Stability

You find a lamp, a genie pops out.
You have 3 wishes. What are they?

(1)

(2)

(3)

Best date night ever...

- Who is on the other side of the restaurant table?:

- Where do you go and what do you do?:

- Where do you eat?:

- Most memorable moment?:

What's the largest animal you could fight
with your bare hands?

Every generation carries the promise of a new world,
what's yours?

How many hours a day do you spend looking at a screen?

Describe your friendship with the book owner
using only verbs (doing words).

Most Likely.

It's like a yearbook but it's better because you actually choose what goes into it.

Write one name for each:

Most likely to be still asked for their ID at 30

Most likely to write a hit song

Most likely to be a teacher

Most likely to go viral

Most likely to break a world record

Most likely to marry a celebrity

Fill this space with a list of things that make you angry.

Finish these sentences...

It breaks my heart when...

I feel guilty that...

I want to...

Describe your personality in 3 words

(1)

(2)

(3)

You're the one that I want:
Choose the top 5 attributes you would look for in a partner:

Lover	○	Fighter	○
Intelligence	○	Sense of Humour	○
Confidence	○	Maturity	○
Authenticity	○	Integrity	○
Affection	○	Fearlessness	○
Empathy	○	Emotional maturity	○
Openness	○	Honesty	○
Uniqueness	○	Sensitivity	○
Respect	○	Responsibility	○
Independence	○	Physical attraction	○
Shared interests	○		

Write a list of 3 places that you would like to live.

(1)

(2)

(3)

You can only choose one. You lose the rest forever.
Circle your choice.

Vinyl   CD   Streaming   Cassette

Doodle a self portrait using only straight lines. The lines can be different sizes and of different thickness.

How united or divided do you feel your generation is?

List 3 things that you are inspired by.

(1)

(2)

(3)

Make a mixtape.
What are the first five tracks on your greatest playlist ever?

(1)

(2)

(3)

(4)

(5)

Doodle hell.

Doodle heaven.

What do you find most ridiculous about previous generations?

Things I will never do (tick those that apply):

Go on a blind date ◯

Lie to a friend ◯

Fire a gun ◯

Get a tattoo ◯

Be a teacher ◯

Join the army ◯

Work at a fast food restaurant ◯

Read a book with no pictures ◯

If you could make one thing in the world disappear right now, what would it be?

List your favourite...

Item of clothing

Place to shop

TV Series

Team

Snack

Animal

What is the number one thing on your bucket list?

What is your favourite quote?

Most Likely.

It's like a yearbook but it's better because you actually choose what goes into it.

Write one name for each:

Most likely to be a celebrity

Most likely to be running the country

Most likely to be a stand-up comedian

Most likely to be Instagram famous

Most likely to win a Nobel Prize

Most likely to be an activist

Either / Or - Circle your choice.

Street Food or Restaurant

No Music for a month or No TV for a month

Wake up late or Go to bed late

Optimism or Realism

Bowling or Go Karting

Expert at one thing or Good at many things

Music Festival or Theatre/Play

Fill this space with a list of things that make you happy.

What is your favourite song lyric?

What happens in the afterlife? (tick your answer):

a) You're reincarnated and born again ◯

b) Your soul moves on to another world ◯

c) You'll go to either heaven or hell ◯
   depending upon your track record

d) Nothing. That's it. You're dead ◯

e) You rejoin the quasi-infinite oneness ◯
   of the carbon cycle

f) Other (please describe) ◯

Write one word here that expresses exactly how you feel right now.

What does the future look like for your generation?

Create a tattoo that summarises your entire identity.

One thing...

You are passionate about

That makes you mad

That you miss

You can't live without

You can keep only 3:

Circle your choices.

Chocolate / Cheese / Tacos / Vegetables / Donuts / Pizza / Burgers / Fried Chicken / Ice Cream / Fruit / French Fries / Pasta / Hot dog / Salad / Cookies / Tofu / Sweets

What is your lucky number?

Doodle a self-portrait in a surrealist style. Look up 'Picasso' and 'Cubism' for reference. Mix it up and put your features in different places.

SOFT SKILLS

Rate yourself out of 10 for each of the following soft skills:

- Emotional Intelligence ◯ out of 10
- Communication ◯ out of 10
- Teamwork ◯ out of 10
- Flexibility ◯ out of 10
- Creativity ◯ out of 10
- Problem Solving ◯ out of 10
- Critical Thinking ◯ out of 10
- Leadership ◯ out of 10
- Time Management ◯ out of 10
- Flirting ◯ out of 10

If you could get a ticket to any show/gig or event in history what would you choose?

If you could live inside anyone's head for a day who would you choose?

BINGO

Read the bingo card. If something is true for you, then put a big cross in the box. If you get a line of four crosses in any direction, shout BINGO!*

Have a job	Don't have a pet	Have a tattoo	Are vegan / vegetarian
Can speak a foreign language	Are allergic to something	Can play an instrument	Hate fast food
Have broken a bone	Don't have a nickname	Have been abroad	Have been on TV
Have been on a blind date	Can't swim	Are left-handed	Have never been skiing

List 3 career/job options that you could imagine doing in the future.

 1

2

3

If you put together your own 'start up' business what would it be called?

*Sorry there is no prize.

Most Likely.

It's like a yearbook but it's better because you actually choose
what goes into it.

Write one name for each:

Most likely to start a cult

Most likely to be a YouTube phenomenon

Most likely to end up in prison

Most likely to marry for money

Most likely to be president

Most likely to be a mad scientist

Doodle a page of hand lettering.

If you could have a walk on part in any movie in history,
what movie would you choose?

SOFT SKILLS
Rate yourself out of 10 for each of the following soft skills:

- Energy, passion and optimism   ◯ out of 10

- Self-confidence   ◯ out of 10

- Creativity and imagination   ◯ out of 10

- Self-control   ◯ out of 10

- Public speaking   ◯ out of 10

- Resilience and persistence   ◯ out of 10

- Sense of humour   ◯ out of 10

**What is the one thing that has happened in the last year that
you will never forget?**

What age should the following be legal?

Driving ◯   Drinking Alcohol ◯

Gun Ownership ◯   Voting ◯

Criminal Responsibility ◯   Marriage ◯

What's your favourite item of clothing?

List your top 3 movies of all time:

(1)

(2)

(3)

Fifty years into the future, what do you think would be the title of your autobiography?

You are asked to DJ at a house party.
What song do you drop to get the party started?

List 10 things on your bucket list:

1.

2.

3.

4.

5.

6.

7.

8.

9.

10.

BINGO

Read the bingo card. If something is true for you, then put a big cross in the box. If you get a line of four crosses in any direction, shout BINGO!*

Have a piercing	Sleep with a stuffed animal	Make a New Year's resolution	Are a member of a club
Have a pet	Believe in reincarnation	Are a night owl	Want a gap year
Have a middle name	Have expensive tastes	Have more than 3 good friends	Prefer animals to people
Have sung karaoke	Been on a blind date	Can cook a 3 course meal	Are an early bird

If you could have a walk-on part in any TV series which one would it be?

Do you always tell the truth? (tick your answer):

- No ⭘
- Yes ⭘
- Mostly, but I might tell the odd white lie now and again ⭘
- I tell people what I think they need to hear ⭘
- What is 'truth' really, when you think about it, hmm? ⭘

*Sorry there is no prize.

Imagine it's time to choose your career and only the following are available, which one do you pick?:

- Fashion Designer ⬚
- Doctor ⬚
- Bartender ⬚
- Zookeeper ⬚
- Police Officer ⬚
- Accountant ⬚
- Taxi Driver ⬚
- Teacher ⬚
- Bounty Hunter ⬚
- Graphic Designer ⬚
- Personal Trainer ⬚
- Lifeguard ⬚
- Psychotherapist ⬚
- Real Estate Agent/Realtor ⬚
- Librarian ⬚

If you and your friends were forming a pop group what would the band be called?

Make up a new dictionary word and describe what that word means.

What food reminds you of home?

Name one person who has had a huge impact on your life.

If you could pick up the phone and call one person living or dead from any time in history who would you call?

Recommend a song.

It's time to predict your future. . . fast forward 20 years':

What object will you still cherish?

Will you be married or single?

Will you have children (if so, how many)?

Where will you live?

What job will you have?

What will your hobby be?

What will be your biggest success?

What will be your biggest failure?

What dream will you realize?

Fill this page with the following doodled items:
Flowers, Donuts, Eyes, Stars, Crowns, Planets, Trees, Beach Balls, Umbrellas, Cacti, Fish, Birds, Suns, Skeletons, Rockets, Lightning, Hearts, Skulls, Daggers, Arrows, Ghosts, Tattoos, Planes, Jellyfish, Lips, Crosses.
Try to fit in as many as possible.

The future is . . .

Give yourself two minutes to look 25 years into the future. Think of all of the things that you think will happen in the news and to the planet. What things will change, what new discoveries might there be and how will society be different?

List your predictions here:

Draw a hand lettered doodle of your favourite
quote/saying/lyric of all time.

Finish this sentence:
My dream is . . .

What is your generation's tragedy?

Either / Or - Circle your choice.

Personality or looks

Order in or Eat Out

Board game or video game

Instagram or Twitter

Couch potato or fitness freak

Animals or people

Start early or Finish late

Call or text

Write down the first four letter word that comes to mind.

Hand illustrate this space with one piece of wisdom or advice.

Sum up the last year in just one word:

They are making a movie of your life story,
what is the movie called?

If you had to give your tribe a name, what would it be?

Rank these in terms of the biggest influences on your
behaviour and actions:

- Generation   ◯
- Regional Identity   ◯
- Ambition   ◯
- Values   ◯
- Level of Education ◯
- Ethnicity   ◯
- Friends   ◯
- Parents   ◯

BINGO

Read the bingo card. If something is true for you, then put a big cross in the box. If you get a line of four crosses in any direction, shout BINGO!*

Have more than one tattoo	Have less than 5 close friends	Have a gym membership (but don't go)	Hate people chewing loudly
Crashed a party	Suffer imposter syndrome	Have cheated on someone	Have been on a plane
Have a gym membership	Have a friend who is 'sketchy'	Are a flexitarian	Have used a fake ID
Been involved in a love triangle	Own a tote bag	Have skipped class at least twice	Have ghosted someone

Either / Or - Circle your choice

Individualism or **Collectivism**

Glass half full or **Glass half empty**

Ambitious or **Laid Back**

Romantic or **Realistic**

Driven by fear of failure or **Motivated by success**

Spontaneity or **Stability**

*Sorry there is no prize.

NOTHING IN THIS LIFE IS MORE IMPORTANT THAN CONNECTING WITH OTHER HUMANS.

Now that you have filled up your time capsule
with the half-mad outpourings of your beloved tribe,
the cake of memory is ready to go into the oven of time.

Every passing year will make it springier
and more delicious.

WHAT NOW?

Bury after writing? You could literally bury it.
Or you could throw it in the attic.

You could deliberately forget about it,
or you could set a little reminder.

Did you know that you can schedule an email
to send yourself in the future?

REPEAT FOREVER?

New chapter, new book, new blank page?
What better way to start out the next adventure
than to embark upon a new group project.

New friends are silver...

LEAVE A REVIEW...

If you loved this book, please leave a review somewhere.

Let's seed the hidden corners of the world
with paper time capsules full of love.

#mypeople   #buryafterwriting